CONTAGIOUS QUOTATIONS

The Little Black Book of Sayings That May Make You Think

MONICA WOFFORD

© Contagious Quotations
Copyright 2005

This book is dedicated to all those seminar

participants and audience members

who have said, "Can we take you home with us?"

And now… you can.

Thank you for always being so eager to get started

and to take what we learn and make it stick!

THE LITTLE BLACK BOOK OF SAYINGS THAT MAY MAKE YOU THINK

Opening Thoughts

Often in classes I find myself coming up with some wild sayings and phrases and I see people madly writing them down, yet am often unable to repeat the brilliance that these participants believe they just heard. Thus, I decided to put them into a book. That was my original motivation at least. The other was that many have said they wished they could take me back to the office with them after a seminar. Many make the choice to have me conduct more training and keynotes speeches at their conferences. For those of you unable to have me come to your office, still want to take me with you, this book was written for you, so that you still can!

This is not to say that I believe any of what I say to be brilliance of my own creation, but as Emory Austin shared with me during one of her talks, "if you sit down at the computer to write at the same time every day, the muses will find you." On many occassions they have found me both at the computer and in the classroom.

These quotations are my thoughts on a variety of different issues, some simple and some complex and some from either one of my books *Contagious Leadership* or *Contagious Customer Service*. Many of them are new additions for which I am abundantly grateful to have been given the gift of being able to articulate them on paper. Enjoy!

To use any of these quotations in your writings or speaking, please request permission to do so at my website www.presentersplus.com or email me directly at Monica@presentersplus.com. I would be happy to hear from you and welcome your feedback.

Monica Wofford is an accomplished speaker, trainer, and author who has touched thousands with her unique message of empowerment and Transformaction™. The author of highly acclaimed CONTAGIOUS LEADERSHIP, *as well as numerous other books, Monica is a sought-after trainer whose presentations change behavior. Her proven strategies, timely techniques, and powerful insights into effective leadership characteristics transform managers into leaders, service people into contagious service providers, and average passer-bys into participants in the game of life. To hire Monica as your next speaker, call 1-866-350-LEAD today!*

TABLE OF
QUOTATIONS

ATTITUDE

"Contagious Charisma comes from sharing
your heart's desire with others."

"Beliefs lead to behaviors which lead to
actions, which lead to results.
To change results, work on beliefs before
behaviors or attitudes."

"Choices are easy. It is the consequences that

can sometimes be a bummer."

"You can be perfect. Just choose when that

is going to be and for how long

then do it perfectly and get over it."

"If your attitude is bad,

Your life will follow.

If your attitude is good,

Your life could be that way,

If you follow up your attitude with actions."

CONTAGIOUS QUOTATIONS

"There can be no contact between an employee and a manager or leader that does not result in the communication of a feeling or attitude."

"A bad attitude is the worst thing that can

happen to a group of people. "

"Managers with a negative attitude are like

monsters whose personality and management

style pervades the entire department

and creates a sense of tension that often

requires surgical removal."

"If you are going to have an attitude,

make it a good one."

"Always try to be positively focused on

what you want and adamantly averse

to those trying to keep you from it."

COMMUNICATION

"Whatever percentage of the message you believe is accurate, this much seems to be true: your body continues talking long after your lips stop moving."

"Communication is a two-way street

on a 6 lane divided highway

with exit ramps every few feet."

"Tell you what, why don't you just tell me

what you mean because my crystal ball

is perpetually in the shop and my

telepathy skills are broken, too."

"You can talk all you want,

but if no one understands you,

the effort and the breath has been wasted."

"Sometimes you learn more by listening

than by talking. In fact, I have learned more

by listening to my inner voices

than I have by talking to myself."

"Considering how different we all are and the
different backgrounds that we have,
the mere fact that anyone is able to
communicate anything to anyone at all
is simply amazing!"

"The question you might ask yourself is this:

When you talk, do people listen?"

"You do talk to yourself, right? If you are not sure of the answer, then finish the conversation in your head and let me know."

"What you say is not anywhere near as
important as how you say it, which is not
anywhere near as important as how
the other person received it."

"There are at least four levels of listening.

Yet, most people are unwilling to spell levels,

much less practice using them effectively."

CONFIDENCE

"Do what you have always wanted to do

with courage and gusto. Your always wanted

to do list comes from your purpose for being."

"Even when you can't see the plan, wouldn't

understand the plan, and aren't sure there

even is a plan in place, confidence

keeps you moving forward."

"Being afraid is far different than lacking confidence. Those with confidence feel the fear and go for it anyway."

(One of Jack Canfield's mantras is "Oh, what the heck, go for it anyway." I just added my take on it.)

"Q: What comes first, food or rent?

A: Neither. What comes first is the belief that you deserve them in abundance followed by the deepest desire to do whatever it takes to make that happen, followed by the sense to be grateful when they come."

"Knowing what to say is good,

knowing when to say it is better,

knowing how to say it,

is best."

"Confidence is doing what you believe is right,

not just what you believe will produce results."

"The whole point of presenting anything

is to connect with your audience

and provide them the information they

requested or you promised!"

"It takes courage to exhibit confidence in
your beliefs and courage to exhibit confidence
in who you believe in."

"Each day I ask confidently 'How can I serve?" and each day I feel confident that I will get an answer. There is no shortage of areas for service in the world."

"Confidently going 200 miles per hour

does not mean you know where you are

going, it means you know how fast

you want to get somewhere."

"How can you believe in someone else

if you don't believe in yourself?"

CUSTOMER SERVICE

"Remember the little things about your customer, even if it is with the help of a database. "

"Everyone out there is your customer.

Therefore customer service is a lifestyle, not a

performance you turn on when you arrive at

work and off when you arrive at home.

Home is not where you go when you are

tired of being nice to people!"

"You are the company to the customer,

so pay attention to what YOU do when in

the presence of your customers."

"If people treated customers like their family,

we would have a much worse customer service

epidemic in this country. However, if people

treated customers like a prospective date,

we would have no issues at all."

"Customers need, want, and

deserve your service. Period."

"Want to know how your customers would

like to be treated? Try this:

ASK THEM."

"If you need more confidence when talking
with an irate customer on the phone, stand
up and at the very least, no matter what,
you will be taller than your caller."

"The customer is so not always right. In fact,

customers lie, steal, cheat and manipulate,

but last time I checked they always BELIEVE

they are correct and that is the point."

"Some days, there are some customers that

I know for a fact, you look at and it is all

you can do to say in your head

'thank heavens I get paid to deal with you'."

"Sometimes you feel like giving good

customer service and sometimes you don't.

It is the times when you don't

that you do, that matter."

GOALS

"If you write your goals down you increase

your chances of achieving them by 50% and

I think that includes cocktail napkins, paper

towels, and scrap pieces of paper.

Write them down!"

"If you spend the time to write down a list for something as mundane and trivial as grocery shopping, why would you not take the time to write down something as important as what you want out of life?"

"A goal is to your life

as a map is to your journey."

"How do you know where to go

if you don't know what you want to see?"

"There are a million and one ways

to do almost anything.

The point is not the how

but the what

and the why."

"I am consistently surprised by how many people have no idea what they want out of life. No wonder so many people feel stuck and victimized and without control. Everyone has control over themselves and their choices. How can we show them that?"

"I watched the neighbor dog for weeks with his goal to get under the fence, scratch away. I watched my horse for a month with her goal of breaking down the fence, kick away. I watch adults all the time, with no goals to break through what are mostly invisible fences, just stand there."

"The more often I hear 'I'll try',

the more it sounds like 'I wish I could,

but don't really think I can'.

Don't try,

DO."

"I am not sure why, but for some reason those
who shouldn't be able to, do amazing things
and those who should be able to do anything,
often chose to do nothing."

"Success comes from confidence and drive,

without a need for control. Confidence is belief

without arrogance. Thus success should

produce one humble, focused person without a

control freak complex.

Where do things go wrong?"

LEADERSHIP

"Share your expectations,

or you will be sharing your feedback,

usually on a mistake and how to fix it."

"Managers track numbers,

such as attendance and absentees.

Leaders get to the heart of the problem."

"Lead others confidently

in ways that serve."

"Many leaders realize that only twenty-five

percent of the population actually appreciates

and understands the value of this phrase:

the bottom line."

"Your business is only as good

as the people who work

WITH

you."

"Leadership is multi-faceted,

just like those who make good leaders,

and the people they serve."

"Leadership includes being able to confidently convey your message AND the ability to confidently convey who you are."

"Leadership is not a gift that everyone is

born with, yet it is a skill that anyone

who wants to can learn.

Pay attention to the want to part."

"Managers have people reporting to them
because of hierarchical structure; leaders have
people following them out of choice.
Begin to treat the people who report to you,
and that you want to follow you, as unique,
and begin to behave like a leader."

"Keep the concept simple:

management works with things,

leadership is much more effective with people."

"If you plan to ascend to leadership

from your position in management,

you have to get up out of your work space

and make some people connections."

LIFE LESSONS

"It isn't what you say, it is how you say it.

This much we know. Yet, we so rarely

put it into practice that the cliché

has almost become cliché."

"'Sometimes you're the statue

and sometimes you are the pigeon'.

The very best part of either is that you always

get to choose each and every day

which one you want to be."

"It is far more difficult to fake what is on our outside, than to fix what is on our inside."

"All of life is a journey. The scenario, terrain,

and destination are all a result of the path

you choose while traveling."

"Are you coming or going... and if you don't

know, at the very least, MOVE."

"Always listen to what is being said;

pay close attention to what is being expressed

through feelings; yet never lose sight for a

moment of what is NOT being said

that you SHOULD be hearing."

"You can't take responsibility

and try to escape it at the same time.

If you did it, you did it; stop trying to deny it,

especially to yourself."

"Do what you say you are going to do

or don't bother doing anything."

"Candor is appreciated

and people say that is what they want.

However, what they mean is tell me the truth,

even if you have to make it up."

RELATIONSHIPS

"The only perfect relationships

I have found, professionally or personally,

were in the movies."

"Relationships take time, nurturing, attention, and effort. We know this to be true about plants, and we do special things for them if we don't want the plant to die, but so many seem to forget to do this with people and wonder why the relationship dies."

"I have heard of the R-generation,

the Relationship era, R-commerce and the

Relationship quotient, but I have yet to see

the same kind of effort to forge relationships

as there is to provide information."

" There is simply something about making a

connection face to face that cannot be

accomplished via email or via the phone,

even a camera phone, and is only enhanced

by the power of touch and eye contact. That

something is magical and not to be ignored."

"If you hang out with the eagles,

you will begin to fly high, the pigeons will

become distant and unfamiliar,

and you will climb higher peaks to reach

higher levels of achievement."

"The best way to build strong relationships

with others is to first build a solid, loving

relationship with yourself. Say nice things to

yourself; treat your body well; fill your mind

with growth and others will be attracted

to the magic that is happening and

the peace you have attained."

"Life is flat out more fun

with a buddy to share it with."

"I am not sure if one can give 110%, but I see plenty who choose to give less than 100% in a relationship. I am not sure if they are a two way street or a multi-lane thoroughfare, but I see plenty who drive down one-way roads and call them relationships. Make no mistake; relationships take work, compromise and the room to make mistakes."

"If you look at the word:

RELATIONSHIP

It is filled with relation and ship.

I think maybe someone was trying to tell us

that relations with other humans will

sometimes encounter smooth sailing and

sometimes encounter rough seas.

Such is the nature of all relationships."

"I think the whole point of communicating is
to make a connection. Why else do people ask
you your name, where do you work and
where you are from and then try to think of
someone that they already know within a
300 mile radius of any of your answers,
only to see if you know them?"

PREFERRED READING LIST
TO INSPIRE MORE THOUGHTS

CONTAGIOUS LEADERSHIP
Monica Wofford

CONTAGIOUS CUSTOMER SERVICE
Monica Wofford

FREE PRIZE INSIDE
Seth Godin

LEADERSHIP BIBLE
John C. Maxwell

SACRED CONTRACTS
Carolyn Myss

SECRETS OF THE MILLIONAIRE MIND
T. Harv Eker

SUCCESS PRINCIPLES
Jack Canfield

THE TIPPING POINT
Malcolm Gladwell

BLINK
Malcolm Gladwell

CONTAGIOUS LEADERSHIP
WITH PRESENTERSPLUS, INCORPORATED

Yes, I *am interested in making the transition from Management to Leadership.*

Please have a PresentersPlus representative contact me by telephone to schedule my Contagious Leadership experience. I would also like to know more about how PresentersPlus can help me to implement the ideas you discuss in Contagious Leadership. I understand that by participating in the Contagious Leadership experience all information that I share will be held in the strictest of confidence.

My key challenges are:

- ☐ Valuing and Respect
- ☐ Taking Interest
- ☐ Asking for Help
- ☐ Micro-Managing
- ☐ Forgiving Mistakes

- ☐ Giving Praise
- ☐ Speaking Clearly
- ☐ Staying Open to Other's Opinions
- ☐ Giving and Accepting Feedback
- ☐ Continuous Improvement

My Name is: ____

My Business address is: Street: ___________________________________

City: _______________________________ State: ______ Zip Code: __________

My E-Mail address is: ____

My Phone number is: ____

My Fax number is: ____

I manage and wish to lead ______ employees, ______ teams, ______ other managers.

I have ______ months or ______ years of management experience.

Here's all you need to do:

You can either fax this completed form to 1-888-877-8366, call us at 1-866-350-LEAD, send an email to monica@presentersplus.com, or mail this completed form to the address below.

P.O. Box 683316 • Orlando, FL 32868

CONTAGIOUS LEADERSHIP
WITH PRESENTERSPLUS, INCORPORATED

Leaders continuously improve. What are you doing to continuously become a better leader and a better person?

Invest In Yourself and Those You Manage:

Contagious Leadership

Additional copies of Contagious Leadership may be purchased at www.createcontagiousleadership.com. Discounts available on group purchases.

Contagious Leadership on AUDIO CD!

Provide those you manage with an instant seminar in their car. Contagious Leadership on audio CD provides 6 CDs of value and templates for completing the journey from management to leadership.

Contagious Confidence on AUDIO CD!

As a leader, one of the greatest challenges you may face is how to convey your message to the people looking to you for guidance. Contagious confidence provides 2 CDs of instruction that will give you the upper edge in presentations and in all communication. Now, you will be heard!

PresentersPlus, Inc., paretn company for Contagious Leadership, founded by Monica Wofford, can help you become a leader and convey your message clearly in any speaking situation. Become the leader you can be with Monica as your speaker, consultant, or coach. To request Monica's services, please call her directly at 1-866-350-LEAD, or send an email to monica@presentersplus.com.

Schedule your Contagious seminar, break-out session, or key note speech today! Don't miss the opportunity to share with those you wish to lead the skills you have found in Contagious Leadership!

P.O. Box 683316 • Orlando, FL 32868

www.ingramcontent.com/pod-product-compliance
Lightning Source LLC
Chambersburg PA
CBHW031314060726

47590CB00003B/1213